AI UNVEILED: A BEGINNERS GUIDE TO UNDERSTANDING ARTIFICIAL INTELLIGENCE

Tonya Roberts

TABLE OF CONTENTS

1. Preface
2. Introduction to AI
3. Chapter 1: The Building Blocks of AI
4. Chapter 2: Types of AI
5. Chapter 3: How AI is Changing the World
6. Chapter 4: The Ethics of AI
7. Chapter 5: Building Your First AI Project
8. Chapter 6: The Future of AI
9. Glossary of AI Terms
10. Further Reading and Resources
11. Acknowledgments

Preface

In the dawn of the digital age, artificial intelligence (AI) stands as both a beacon of promise and a topic of debate. "AI Unveiled: A Beginner's Guide to Understanding Artificial Intelligence" is crafted with the vision of demystifying AI for those who stand curious at its threshold. This book is for students, professionals, and everyday readers who seek to understand the fundamentals of AI and its implications for the future.

I extend my deepest gratitude to the myriad of individuals whose work in the field of AI has paved the way for books like this. May this guide serve as a compass for navigating the complex and ever-evolving landscape of artificial intelligence.

INTRODUCTION TO AI

Welcome to "AI Unveiled," where we embark on a journey through the realms of artificial intelligence. AI, once the domain of science fiction, now touches our daily lives in more ways than we can count. From the recommendations on your favorite streaming service to the virtual assistant in your smartphone, AI's influence is ubiquitous and growing. This book aims to peel back the layers of AI, offering a clear understanding of its mechanisms, applications, and future directions.

CHAPTER 1

THE BUILDING BLOCKS OF AI

Artificial Intelligence (AI) is a branch of computer science dedicated to creating systems capable of performing tasks that typically require human intelligence. These tasks include learning, problem-solving, decision-making, and understanding natural language. Unlike traditional computer programs that follow strict rules, AI systems learn from data, identifying patterns and making decisions with minimal human intervention.

Brief History of AI

The concept of artificial intelligence is not new. Its roots can be traced back to ancient myths and stories of artificial beings endowed with intelligence or consciousness by master craftsmen. However, the scientific pursuit of AI began in earnest in the mid-20th century.

- **1950s**: The term "Artificial Intelligence" was coined in 1956 by John McCarthy, a computer scientist, at the Dartmouth Conference. The project proposal for this conference asserted that "every aspect of learning or any other feature of intelligence can in principle be so precisely described that a machine can be made to simulate it."
- **1960s to 1970s**: Early AI research focused on problem-solving and symbolic methods. The period saw the creation of the first AI programs, including ones that could play checkers and solve algebra problems.
- **1980s to 1990s**: The advent of machine learning, where computers were designed to learn from and make

decisions based on data, marked a shift in AI research. This era also saw the development of neural networks, a type of AI inspired by the human brain's architecture.

- **2000s to Present**: Today, AI has advanced significantly, powered by exponential increases in computing power and data availability. Deep learning, a subset of machine learning involving neural networks with many layers, has led to breakthroughs in image and speech recognition, natural language processing, and more.

Demystifying AI: Separating Fact from Fiction

AI often conjures images of sentient robots and superintelligent systems that surpass human capabilities. While AI has made incredible strides, current technologies are still far from achieving the self-awareness and general intelligence seen in science fiction.

Today's AI excels at performing specific tasks, known as Narrow AI. These systems can outperform humans in their designated tasks, such as playing chess or analyzing medical images, but they lack the understanding and general intelligence to perform beyond their programming.

Understanding AI's Impact

As we stand on the brink of what many call the Fourth Industrial Revolution, AI's impact on our lives is undeniable. It has the potential to solve complex problems in healthcare, environmental protection, and many other fields. However, it also raises ethical questions and challenges, including job displacement and privacy concerns.

In this book, we aim to explore all these facets of AI. By understanding AI's principles, history, applications, and implications, we can better prepare ourselves for a future in which AI plays an increasingly central role.

CHAPTER 2

TYPES OF AI

Artificial intelligence can be broadly categorized into three types based on its capabilities: Narrow AI, General AI, and Superintelligent AI.

Narrow AI

Also known as Weak AI, Narrow AI refers to systems that are designed and trained for a specific task. Examples include facial recognition systems, internet search engines, and self-driving cars. These AI systems are excellent at performing the tasks they are designed for but cannot operate beyond those tasks.

General AI

General AI, or Strong AI, refers to a system with generalized human cognitive abilities. When presented with an unfamiliar task, a General AI system can find a solution without human intervention, much like a human would. This type of AI remains theoretical and has not yet been achieved.

Superintelligent AI

Superintelligent AI surpasses human intelligence and capabilities in every field, including creativity, general wisdom, and social skills. The concept of superintelligent AI is still speculative, with significant debate about its feasibility and the ethical implications of its potential development.

CHAPTER 3

HOW AI IS CHANGING THE WORLD

I is already transforming various sectors by enhancing efficiency, accuracy, and capabilities.

Healthcare

AI applications in healthcare range from predictive analytics for disease outbreaks to personalized treatment plans based on genetic information. AI-driven diagnostic tools are improving the accuracy and speed of disease detection.

Finance

In the finance sector, AI algorithms are used for fraud detection, risk management, and automated trading. AI systems analyze large datasets to detect patterns and predict market trends, providing a competitive edge in financial decision-making.

Education

AI is personalizing education through adaptive learning systems that cater to individual student needs. These systems analyze student performance data to tailor

educational content and provide targeted support, enhancing learning outcomes.

Transportation

Autonomous vehicles are one of the most visible applications of AI in transportation. AI technologies enable self-driving cars to navigate, avoid obstacles, and follow traffic rules, promising to reduce accidents and improve traffic flow.

Customer Service

AI-powered chatbots and virtual assistants are transforming customer service by providing instant, 24/7 support. These systems use natural language processing to understand and respond to customer queries, improving user experience and operational efficiency.

CHAPTER 4

THE ETHICS OF AI

The rapid advancement of AI brings several ethical considerations that must be addressed to ensure responsible development and deployment.

Bias and Fairness

AI systems can inadvertently perpetuate or exacerbate biases present in their training data. Ensuring fairness in AI involves developing methods to detect and mitigate bias, promoting transparency, and involving diverse perspectives in AI development.

Privacy

AI technologies often rely on large amounts of data, raising concerns about privacy and data security. Establishing robust data protection regulations and practices is essential to safeguard individual privacy while leveraging AI's potential.

Accountability

As AI systems become more autonomous, determining accountability for their actions becomes challenging. Developing frameworks for AI accountability involves defining responsibility, establishing standards, and ensuring that AI developers and users adhere to ethical guidelines.

Job Displacement

AI has the potential to automate tasks traditionally performed by humans, leading to job displacement in various sectors. Addressing this issue involves investing in education and training programs to prepare the workforce for AI-driven changes and exploring policies to support those affected by automation.

CHAPTER 5

BUILDING YOUR FIRST AI PROJECT

Creating your first AI project can be an exciting and rewarding experience. Here's a step-by-step guide to get you started.

Step 1: Define the Problem

Identify a specific problem that you want to solve with AI. This could be anything from predicting stock prices to creating a recommendation system for a website.

Step 2: Gather Data

Collect relevant data for your project. High-quality data is crucial for training effective AI models. Ensure that your data is clean, well-organized, and representative of the problem you are trying to solve.

Step 3: Choose the Right Tools

Select the appropriate tools and frameworks for your AI project. Popular choices include TensorFlow, PyTorch, and scikit-learn, each offering different features suited to various types of AI development.

Step 4: Preprocess the Data

Prepare your data for training by cleaning, normalizing, and splitting it into training and testing sets. Data preprocessing is a critical step that can significantly impact your model's performance.

Step 5: Build and Train the Model

Choose a suitable AI model for your problem and train it using your preprocessed data. This involves selecting the right algorithms, tuning hyperparameters, and iteratively testing and improving your model.

Step 6: Evaluate and Optimize

Evaluate your model's performance using appropriate metrics and refine it as needed. This may involve adjusting the model's architecture, retraining with additional data, or fine-tuning hyperparameters.

Step 7: Deploy the Model

Once your model is ready, deploy it to a production environment where it can start solving real-world problems. Monitor its performance and make updates as necessary to ensure it continues to perform effectively.

CHAPTER 6

THE FUTURE OF AI

The future of AI holds immense potential, with ongoing research and development pushing the boundaries of what is possible.

Advancements in AI Research

Emerging areas of AI research include quantum computing, neuromorphic engineering, and advanced machine learning techniques. These advancements promise to enhance AI's capabilities and open new frontiers in technology.

Quantum Computing

Quantum computing leverages the principles of quantum mechanics to perform computations at unprecedented speeds. Unlike classical computers, which use bits as the smallest unit of data, quantum computers use quantum bits or qubits. These qubits can exist in multiple states simultaneously, allowing quantum computers to process vast amounts of data and solve complex problems much faster than traditional computers. This breakthrough has significant implications for AI, particularly in areas such as cryptography, drug discovery, and optimization problems.

Neuromorphic Engineering

Neuromorphic engineering involves designing computer systems inspired by the human brain's architecture. These systems use specialized hardware to emulate the brain's neural structure and functioning, enabling more efficient and powerful AI computations. Neuromorphic chips can process information in parallel, consume less energy, and adapt to new data more quickly than traditional processors. This technology promises to bring AI closer to human-like cognitive abilities.

Advanced Machine Learning Techniques

Advancements in machine learning techniques, such as reinforcement learning, generative adversarial networks (GANs), and transfer learning, are expanding AI's capabilities. Reinforcement learning enables AI systems to learn by interacting with their environment and receiving feedback, making it ideal for applications like robotics and game playing. GANs consist of two neural networks that compete against each other to generate realistic data, leading to breakthroughs in image and video synthesis. Transfer learning allows AI models to apply knowledge gained from one task to different but related tasks, reducing the amount of data and training time required for new applications.

AI and Society

As AI becomes more integrated into society, its impact on various aspects of life will continue to grow. Understanding and preparing for these changes is crucial to harnessing AI's potential while mitigating its risks.

Economic Impact

AI is poised to drive significant economic growth by enhancing productivity, creating new industries, and transforming existing ones. However, it also raises concerns about job displacement and income inequality. To address these challenges, policymakers, businesses, and educational institutions must collaborate to create a future workforce equipped with the skills needed in an AI-driven economy. This includes investing in STEM education, lifelong learning programs, and policies that support workers transitioning between jobs.

Ethical and Legal Considerations

The ethical and legal implications of AI are profound. As AI systems become more autonomous, ensuring they operate fairly, transparently, and responsibly becomes increasingly important. Establishing comprehensive regulatory frameworks, ethical guidelines, and accountability mechanisms is essential to prevent misuse and protect individual rights. Additionally, fostering public awareness and engagement in discussions about AI ethics can help shape policies that reflect societal values and priorities.

Human-AI Collaboration

The future of AI will likely involve increased collaboration between humans and AI systems. AI can augment human capabilities by automating routine tasks, providing insights from vast data sets, and assisting in decision-making processes. This collaboration can lead to more efficient workflows, better outcomes in various fields, and new opportunities for innovation. Emphasizing the development of user-friendly AI tools and fostering a culture of collaboration can maximize the benefits of human-AI partnerships.

GLOSSARY OF AI TERMS

- **Algorithm**: A step-by-step procedure or formula for solving a problem.
- **Artificial Intelligence (AI)**: The simulation of human intelligence processes by machines, especially computer systems.
- **Big Data**: Extremely large data sets that may be analyzed computationally to reveal patterns, trends, and associations.
- **Deep Learning**: A subset of machine learning involving neural networks with many layers that can learn from large amounts of data.
- **Machine Learning (ML)**: A type of AI that allows software applications to become more accurate at predicting outcomes without being explicitly programmed.
- **Neural Network**: A series of algorithms that attempt to recognize underlying relationships in a set of data through a process that mimics the way the human brain operates.
- **Natural Language Processing (NLP)**: A branch of AI that helps computers understand, interpret, and respond to human language.
- **Qubit**: The basic unit of quantum information, which can represent both 0 and 1 simultaneously due to the principles of quantum mechanics.
- **Reinforcement Learning**: A type of machine learning where an agent learns to make decisions by taking actions in an environment to maximize cumulative reward.
- **Supervised Learning**: A type of machine learning where an algorithm is trained on labeled data.

FURTHER READING AND RESOURCES

For those interested in diving deeper into the world of AI, the following resources provide comprehensive information and learning opportunities:

Books
- "Artificial Intelligence: A Modern Approach" by Stuart Russell and Peter Norvig.
- "Deep Learning" by Ian Goodfellow, Yoshua Bengio, and Aaron Courville
- "Life 3.0: Being Human in the Age of Artificial Intelligence" by Max Tegmark

ONLINE COURSES

- Coursera: Machine Learning by Andrew Ng
- edX: Artificial Intelligence by Columbia University
- Udacity: Deep Learning Nanodegree

WEBSITES AND BLOGS

- Towards Data Science (towardsdatascience.com)
- OpenAI (openai.com)
- The AI Alignment Forum (alignmentforum.org)

RESEARCH PAPERS AND JOURNALS

- "Nature Machine Intelligence"
- "Journal of Artificial Intelligence Research"
- "IEEE Transactions on Neural Networks and Learning Systems"

ACKNOWLEDGMENTS

Creating this book has been a collaborative effort, and I am grateful to everyone who contributed to its completion. I would like to thank the researchers, engineers, and thought leaders in the field of AI whose work has provided the foundation for this book. Special thanks to my editor for their invaluable feedback and guidance, and to my family for their unwavering support and encouragement. Lastly, I extend my gratitude to the readers who inspire the continuous exploration and understanding of artificial intelligence.

www.ingramcontent.com/pod-product-compliance
Lightning Source LLC
Chambersburg PA
CBHW072058230526
45479CB00010B/1131